Steve a

Written by Ma

Illustrated by Ite Kano

Short e (CVC words)		**Long e (VCe words)**
gets	men	Pete
help	net	Steve
helps	pets	

High-Frequency Words

black	down	know	this	were
brown	how	they	two	white

Steve and Pete help.

They know how to drive safe.

Two men were stuck in a net.

Steve and Pete help the men.

Steve helps the black pup.
Steve helps the brown pup.
Steve gets the pets down.

Pete helps a white cat.
He finds her home.

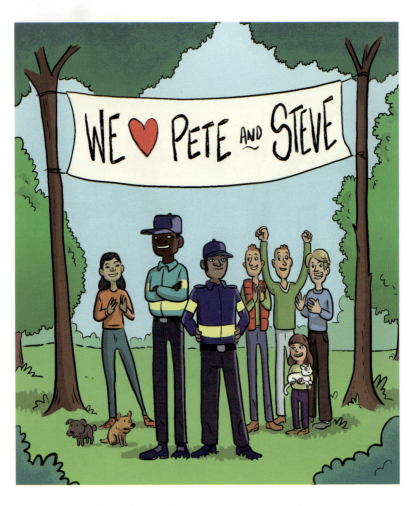

We made this for Steve and Pete.